INDIA

INDIA

SWAMI VIVEKANANDA

GYAN

Published by

Gyan Publishing House
5, Ansari Road
Daryaganj, New Delhi-110002
Phone: 011-47034999, 9811692060
E-mail: books@gyanbooks.com

Distribution Network
gyanbooks.com
India, USA, Canada, UK, Australia

ISBN: 978-93-7225-137-1 (PB)

First Published, 1947

2nd Impression 2025

Printed at: Gyan Press, Delhi.

INDIA
Author: SWAMI VIVEKANANDA

INDIA

SWAMI VIVEKANANDA

INDIA

BY

SWAMI VIVEKANANDA

ADVAITA ASHRAMA
MAYAVATI, ALMORA, HIMALAYAS

PREFACE

Very few have known India so thoroughly as did Swami Vivekananda, and it may be said, without any fear of contradiction, that very few have loved India with the same degree of intensity as he did. Once Swami Vivekananda asked : You talk of patriotism, but has the thought of your motherland taken so much hold of you, that you have lost your sleep and you carry the burden of the misery of your people throughout your waking moments ? That is real patriotism. Those who are acquainted with the life story of Swami Vivekananda know that he had this kind of patriotism.

There are some people in our country whose love for India is great and who are also ready to implement that love in service and self-sacrifice, but unfortunately they themselves are strangers to their own country. They have not known what real India is ; they are, as it were, not rooted in the soil of the country. To know real India you must know her ancient culture ; you must know the people and identify yourself with their hopes and aspirations, joys and sorrows, and with their daily problems. Swamiji was unique in this respect. He had not only an intellectual grasp of the cultural heritage of India, born of deep study, hard thinking and keen observation, but he had also direct realisations of the spiritual truths for which India stands. He was a saint and a patriot in one. And, above all, as a wandering monk, moving from one corner of the country to the other, mixing with the high and the low, the prince and the peasant, the educated and the unlettered, he saw with his own eyes, how the heart beats of ancient India persist even through the apparent degradation of the present days, and how India bears ever in her bosom the spark of divine fire which under favourable conditions is likely to blaze up again. As such, Swami Vivekananda was the fittest person to talk on India and give guidance to the workers engaged in the task of moulding her destiny. Here in the following pages are collected some of the writings of Swami Vivekananda dealing with India. They may be found very useful at a time when India is entering on a new era of her history.

PUBLISHER

ADVAITA ASHRAMA
MAYAVATI, HIMALAYAS
April 24, 1947

CON EENTS

INDIA

INDIA'S MESSAGE TO THE WORLD

The following notes were discovered among Swami Vivekananda's papers. He intended to write a book and jotted down forty-two points as a syllabus for the work, but only a few points were dealt with as an introduction by him and the work was left unfinished. We give the manuscripts as found.

The Syllabus

1. Bold has been my message to the people of the West. Bolder to those at home.
2. Four years of residence in the marvellous West has made India only the better understood. The shades are deeper and the lights brighter.
3. The survey—it is not true that the Indians have degenerated.
4. The problem here has been as it has been everywhere else—the assimilation of various races, but nowhere has it been so vast as here.
5. Community of language, government

and, above all, religion has been the power of fusion.

6. In other lands this has been attempted by "force," that is, the enforcement of the culture of one *race* only over the rest. The result being the production of a shortlived vigorous national life ; then, dissolution.

7. In India, on the other hand, the attempts have been as gentle as the problem vast, and from the earliest times, the customs, and especially the religions, of the different elements tolerated.

8. Where it was a small problem and force was sufficient to form a unity, the effect really was the nipping in the bud of various healthy types in the germ of all the elements except the dominant one. It was only one set of brains using the vast majority for its own good, thus losing the major portion of the possible amount of development, and thus when the dominant type had spent itself, the apparently impregnable building tottered to its ruins, e.g., Greece, Rome, the Norman.

9. A common language would be a great

desideratum, but the same criticism applies to it, the destruction of the vitality of the various existing ones.

10. The only solution to be reached was the finding of a great sacred language of which all the others would be considered as manifestations, and that was found in the Sanskrit.

11. The Dravidian languages may or may not have been originally Sanskritic, but for practical purposes they are so now, and every day we see them approaching the ideal more and more, yet keeping their distinctive vital peculiarities.

12. A racial background was found—the Aryas.

13. The speculation whether there was a distinct, separate race called the Aryas living in Central Asia to the Baltic.

14. The so-called types. Races were always mixed.

15. The "blonde" and the "brunette."

16. Coming to practical common sense from so-called historical imagination. The Aryas in their oldest records were in the land between

Turkistan and the Punjab and N. W. Thibet.

17. This leads to the attempt at fusion between races and tribes of various degrees of culture.

18. Just as Sanskrit has been the linguistic solution, so the Arya the racial solution. So the Brahminhood is the solution of the varying degrees of progress and culture as well as that of all social and political problems.

19. The great ideal of India—Brahminhood.

20. Property-less, selfless, subject to no laws, no king except the moral.

21. Brahminhood by descent—various races have claimed and acquired the right in the past as well as in the present.

22. No claim is made by the doer of great deeds, only by lazy worthless fools.

23. Degradation of Brahminhood and Kshatriyahood. The Puranas said there will be only non-Brahmins in the Kali Yuga, and that is true, becoming truer every day. Yet a few Brahmins remain, and in India alone.

24. Kshatriyahood—we must pass through that to become a Brahmin. Some may have

passed through in the past, but the present must show that.

25. But the disclosure of the whole plan is to be found in religion.

26. The different tribes of the same race worship similar gods, under a generic name as the Bels of the Babylonians, the Molochs of the Hebrews.

27. The attempt in Babylonia of making all the Bels merge in Bel-Merodach—the attempt of the Israelites to merge all the Molochs in the Moloch Yavah or Yahu.

28. The Babylonians destroyed by the Persians, and the Hebrews who took the Babylonian mythology and adapted it to their own needs, succeeded in producing a strict monotheistic religion.

29. Monotheism like absolute monarchy is quick in executing orders, and a great centralisation of force, but it grows no farther, and its worst feature is its cruelty and persecution. All nations coming within its influence perish very soon after a flaring up of a few years.

30. In India the same problem presented

itself—the solution found—एकं सद्विप्रा बहुधा वदन्ति ।

This is the keynote to everything which has succeeded, and the keystone of the arch.

31. The result is that wonderful toleration of the Vedantist.

32. The great problem therefore is to harmonise and unify without destroying the individuality of these various elements.

33. No form of religion which depends upon persons, either of this earth or even of heaven, is able to do that.

34. Here is the glory of the Advaita system preaching a principle, not a person, yet allowing persons, both human and divine, to have their full play.

35. This has been going on all the time; in this sense we have been always progressing. The Prophets during the Mohammedan rule.

36. It was fully conscious and vigorous in old days, and less so of late; in this sense alone we have degenerated.

37. This is going to be in the future. If the manifestation of the power of one tribe utilising the labours of the rest produced

wonderful results at least for a certain length of time, here is going to be the accumulation and the concentration of all the races that have been slowly and inevitably getting mixed up in blood and ideas, and in my mind's eye, I see the future giant slowly maturing. The future India, the youngest and the most glorious of the nations of earth as well as the oldest.

38. The way—we will have to work. Social customs as barriers, some as founded upon the Smritis. But none from the Shrutis. The Smritis must change with time. This is the admitted law.

39. The principles of the Vedanta not only should be preached everywhere in India, but also outside. Our thought must enter into the make-up of the minds of every nation, not through writings, but through persons.

40. Gift is the only Karma in Kali Yuga. None attaining knowledge until purified by Karma.

41. Gift of spiritual and secular knowledge.

42. Renunciation—Renouncers—the national call.

Introduction

Bold has been my message to the people of the West, bolder is my message to you, my beloved countrymen. The message of ancient India to new Western nations I have tried my best to voice—ill done or well done the future is sure to show, but the mighty voice of the same future is already sending forward soft but distinct murmurs, gaining strength as the days go by, the message of India that is to be to India as she is at present.

Many wonderful institutions and customs, and many wonderful manifestations of strength and power it has been my good fortune to study in the midst of the various races I have seen, but the most wonderful of all was to find that beneath all these apparent variations of manners and customs, of culture and power, beats the same mighty human heart under the impulsion of the same joys and sorrows, of the same weakness and strength.

Good and evil are everywhere and the balance is wondrously even, but above all is the glorious soul of man everywhere which never fails to understand anyone who knows how to speak its own language. Men and women are to be found in every race whose lives are blessings to humanity, verifying the words of the Divine Emperor Ashoka—"In every land dwell Brahmins and Shramanas."

I am grateful to the lands of the West for the many warm hearts that received me with all the love that pure and disinterested souls alone could give, but my life's allegiance is to this my Motherland, and if I had a thousand lives, every moment of the whole series would be consecrated to your service, my countrymen, my friends.

For to this land I owe whatever I possess, physical, mental and spiritual, and if I have been successful in anything, the glory is yours, not mine. Mine alone are my weaknesses and failures, as they come through my inability of profiting by the mighty lessons with which this land surrounds one, even from his very birth.

And what a land! Whosoever stands on this sacred land, whether alien or a child of the soil, feels himself surrounded—unless his soul is degraded to the level of brute animals—by the living thoughts of the earth's best and purest sons, who have been working to raise the animal to the Divine through centuries, whose beginning history fails to trace. The very air is full of the pulsations of spirituality. This land is sacred to philosophy, to ethics and spirituality, to all that tends to give a respite to man in his incessant struggle for the preservation of the animal, to all training that makes man throw off the garment of brutality and stand revealed as the Spirit immortal, the birthless, the deathless, the ever-blessed—the land where the cup of pleasure was full, and fuller has been the cup of misery, until here, first of all, man found out that it was all vanity ; here, first of all, in the prime of youth, in the lap of luxury, in the height of glory and plenitude of power, he broke through the fetters of delusion. Here in this ocean of humanity, amidst the sharp interaction of strong currents of pleasure and pain, of strength and weakness, of wealth and poverty, of joy and sorrow, of smile and tear, of life and death, in the melting rhythm of eternal peace and calmness, arose the throne of renunciation ! Here in this land, the great problems of life and death, of the thirst for life, and the vain mad struggles to preserve it only resulting in the accumulation of woes, were first grappled with and solved—solved as they never were before and never will be hereafter ; for here, and here alone was discovered, that even life itself is an evil, the shadow only of something which alone is real. This is the land where alone religion was practical and real, and here alone men and women plunged boldly in to realise the goal, just as in other lands, they madly plunge in to realise the pleasures of life, by robbing their weaker brethren. Here, and here, alone the human heart expanded till it included not only the human, but birds, beasts, and plants ; from the highest gods to grains of sand, the highest and the lowest, all find a place in the heart of man, grown great, infinite. And here alone, the human soul studied the universe as one unbroken unity whose every pulse was his own pulse.

We all hear so much about the degradation of India. There was a time when I also believed in it. But to-day standing on the vantage-ground of experience, with eyes cleared of obstructive predispositions and above all, of the highly-coloured pictures of other countries toned down to their proper shade and light by actual contact, I confess, in all humility, that I was wrong. Thou blessed land of the Aryas, thou wast never degraded. Sceptres have been broken and thrown away, the ball of power has passed from hand to hand, but in India, courts and kings always touched only a few ; the vast mass of the people, from the highest to the lowest, has been left to pursue its own inevitable course, the current of national life flowing at times slow and half-conscious, at others, strong and awakened. I stand in awe before the unbroken procession of scores of shining centuries, with here and there a dim link in the chain, only to flare up with added brilliance in the next, and there she is walking with her own majestic steps—my motherland—to fulfil her glorious destiny, which no power on earth or in heaven can check—the regeneration of man the brute into man the God.

Aye, a glorious destiny, my brethren, for as far back as the days of the Upanishads we have thrown the challenge to the world— न धनेन न प्रजया त्यागेनैके अमृतत्वमानशुः । "Not by wealth, not by progeny, but by renunciation alone immortality is reached." Race after race has taken the challenge up, and tried their utmost to solve the world-riddle on the plane of desires. They have all failed in the past—the old ones have become extinct under the weight of wickedness and misery, which lust for power and gold brings in its train, and the new ones are tottering to their fall. The question has yet to be decided whether peace will survive or war; whether patience will survive or non-forbearance, whether goodness will survive or wickedness; whether muscle will survive or brain; whether worldliness will survive or spirituality. We have solved our problem ages ago, and held on to it through good or evil fortune, and mean to hold on to it till the end of time. Our solution is unworldliness—renunciation.

This is the theme of Indian life-work, the burden of her eternal songs, the backbone of her existence, the foundation of her being, the *raison d'etre* of her very existence—the spiritualisation of the human race. In this her life-course she has never deviated, whether the Tartar ruled or the Turk, whether the Mogul ruled or the English.

And I challenge anybody to show one single period of her national life when India was lacking in spiritual giants, capable of moving the world. But her work is spiritual, and that cannot be done with blasts of war-trumpets or the march of cohorts. Her influence has always fallen upon the world like that of the gentle dew, unheard and scarcely marked, yet bringing into bloom the fairest flowers of the earth. This influence being in its nature gentle, would have to wait for a fortunate combination of circumstances, to go out of the country into other lands, though it never ceased to work within the limits of its native land. As such, every educated person knows that whenever the empire-building Tartar or Persian or Greek or Arab brought this land in contact with the outside world, a mass of spiritual influence immediately flooded the world from here. The very same circumstances have presented themselves once more before us. The English high-roads over land and sea and the wonderful power manifested by the inhabitants of that little island, have once more brought India in contact with the rest of the world, and the same work has already begun. Mark my words, this is but the small beginning, big things are to follow ; what the result of the present work outside India will be I cannot exactly state, but this I know for certain, that millions, I say deliberately, millions in every civilised land are waiting for the message that will save them from the hideous abyss of materialism into which modern money-worship is driving them headlong, and many of the leaders of the new social movements have already discovered, that Vedanta in its highest form can alone spiritualise their social aspirations. I shall have to return to this towards the end. I take up therefore the other great subject, the work within the country.

The problem assumes a twofold aspect, not only spiritualisation but assimilation of the various elements of which the nation is composed. The assimilation of different races into one, has been the common task in the life of every nation.

INDIAN RELIGIOUS THOUGHT

(Delivered under the auspices of the Brooklyn Ethical Society, in the Art Gallery of the Pouch Mansion, Clinton Avenue, Brooklyn, U. S. A.)

India, although only half the size of the United States, contains a population of over two hundred and ninety millions, and there are three religions which hold sway over them, the Mohammedan, the Buddhist[1] and the Hindu. The adherents of the first mentioned number about sixty millions, of the second, about nine millions, while the last embrace nearly two hundred and six millions. The cardinal features of the Hindu religion are founded on the meditative and speculative philosophy and on the ethical teachings contained in the various books of the Vedas, which assert that the universe is infinite in space and eternal in duration. It never had a beginning, and it never will have an end. Innumerable have been the manifestations of the power of

[1] Including the Jain.

the Spirit in the realm of matter, of the force of the Infinite in the domain of the finite, but the Infinite Spirit Itself is self-existent, eternal and unchangeable. The passage of time makes no mark whatever on the dial of eternity. In Its supersensuous region which cannot be comprehended at all by the human understanding, there is no past, and there is no future. The Vedas teach that the soul of man is immortal. The body is subject to the law of growth and decay ; what grows, must of necessity decay. But the in-dwelling Spirit is related to the infinite and eternal life ; it never had a beginning and it never will have an end. One of the chief distinctions between the Hindu and the Christian religion is, that the Christian religion teaches that each human soul had its beginning, at its birth into this world ; whereas the Hindu religion asserts, that the Spirit of man is an emanation of the Eternal Being, and had no more a beginning than God Himself. Innumerable have been and will be its manifestations in its passage from one personality to another, subject to the great law of spiritual evolution, until it reaches perfection, when there is no more change.

It has been often asked, if this be so, why is it we do not remember anything of our past lives? This is our explanation: Consciousness is the name of the surface only of the mental ocean; but within its depths are stored up all our experiences, both pleasant and painful. The desire of the human soul is to find out something that is stable. The mind and the body, in fact all the various phenomena of Nature are in a condition of incessant change. But the highest aspiration of our spirit is to find out something that does not change, that has reached a state of permanent perfection. And this is the aspiration of the human soul after the Infinite! The finer our moral and intellectual development, the stronger will become this aspiration after the Eternal that changes not.

The modern Buddhists teach that everything that cannot be known by the five senses is non-existent, and that it is a delusion to suppose that man is an independent entity. The idealists, on the contrary, claim that each individual is an independent entity, and the external world does not exist outside of his mental conception. But the sure solution of this problem is, that Nature is a mixture of independence and dependence, of reality and idealism. Our mind and bodies are dependent on the external world and this dependence varies according to the nature of their relation to it ; but the indwelling Spirit is free, as God is free, and is able to direct in a greater or lesser degree, according to the state of their development, the movements of our minds and bodies.

Death is but a change of condition. We remain in the same universe, and are subject to the same laws as before. Those who have passed beyond, and have attained high planes of development in beauty and wisdom, are but the advance-guard of a universal army, who are following after them. The spirit of the highest is related to the spirit of the lowest, and the germ of infinite perfection exists in all.

We should cultivate the optimistic temperament, and endeavour to see the good that dwells in everything. If we sit down and lament over the imperfection of our bodies and minds, we profit nothing ; it is the heroic endeavour to subdue adverse circumstances that carries our spirits upwards. The object of life is to learn the laws of spiritual progress. Christians can learn from Hindus, and Hindus can learn from Christians. Each has made a contribution of value to the wisdom of the world.

Impress upon your children that true religion is positive, and not negative. That it does not consist in merely refraining from evil, but in a persistent performance of noble deeds. True religion comes not from the teaching of men or the reading of books ; it is the awakening of the Spirit within us, consequent upon pure and heroic action. Every child born into the world brings with it a certain accumulated experience from previous incarnations and the impress of this experience is seen in the structure of its mind and body. But the feeling of independence which possesses us all, shows there is something in us besides mind and body. The soul that reigns within is independent, and creates the desire for freedom. If we are not free, how can we hope to make the world better? We hold that human progress is the result of the action of the human Spirit. What the world is, and what we ourselves are, are the fruits of the freedom of the Spirit.

We believe in one God, the Father of us all, who is omnipresent, and omnipotent, and who guides and preserves His children with infinite love. We believe in a Personal God as the Christians do, but we go further; we believe that we are He! That His personality is manifested in us, that God is in us, and that we are in God. We believe there is a germ of truth in all religions, and the Hindu bows down to them all; for, in this world, truth is to be found not in subtraction but in addition. We would offer God a bouquet of the most beautiful flowers of all the diverse faiths. We must love God for love's sake, not for the hope of reward. We must do our duty for duty's sake, not for the hope of reward. We must worship the beautiful for beauty's sake, not for the hope of reward. Thus in the purity of our hearts shall we see God. Sacrifices, genuflexions, mumblings and mutterings are not religion. They are only good if they stimulate us to the brave performance of beautiful and heroic deeds, and lift our thoughts to the apprehension of the divine perfection.

What good is it, if we acknowledge in our prayers that God is the Father of us all, and in our daily lives do not treat every man as our brother? Books are only made so that they may point the way to a higher life, but no good results, unless the path is trodden with unflinching steps! Every human personality may be compared to a glass globe. There is the same pure white light—an emission of the divine Being—in the centre of each, but the glass being of different colours and thickness, the rays assume diverse aspects in the transmission. The equality and beauty of each central flame is the same, and the apparent inequality is only in the imperfection of the temporal instrument of its expression. As we rise higher and higher in the scale of being, the medium becomes more and more translucent.

ON ART IN INDIA

"Arts and Sciences in India" was the topic under which the Swami Vivekananda was introduced to the audience at Wendte Hall, San Francisco. The Swami held the attention of his hearers throughout as was demonstrated by the many questions which were put to him after his address.

The Swami said in part :

In the history of nations, the government, at the beginning, has always been in the hands of the priests. All the learning also has proceeded from the priests. Then, after the priests, the government changes hands, and the Kshatriya or the kingly power prevails, and the military rule is triumphant. This has always been true. And last comes the grasp of luxury, and the people sink down under it to be dominated by stronger and more barbarous races.

Amongst all races of the world, from the earliest time in history, India has been called the land of wisdom. For ages India itself has never gone out to conquer other nations. Its people have never been fighters. Unlike your Western people, they do not eat meat, for meat makes fighters ; the blood of animals makes you restless and you desire to do something.

Compare India and England in the Elizabethan period. What a dark age it was for your people and how enlightened we were even then. The Anglo-Saxon people have always been badly fitted for art. They have good poetry—for instance, how wonderful is the blank verse of Shakespeare. Merely the rhyming of words is not good ; it is the most uncivilised thing in the world.

In India, music was developed to the full seven notes : even to half and quarter notes, ages ago. India led in music, also in drama and sculpture. Whatever is done now is merely an attempt at imitation. Everything now in India hinges on the question of how little a man requires to live upon.

IS INDIA A BENIGHTED COUNTRY ?

The following is a report of a lecture at Detroit, United States, America, with the editorial comments of the *Boston Evening Transcript,* 5th April, 1894 :

Swami Vivekananda has been in Detroit recently and made a profound impression there. All classes flocked to hear him, and professional men in particular were greatly interested in his logic and his soundness of thought. The opera-house alone was large enough for his audience. He speaks English extremely well, and he is as handsome as he is good. The Detroit newspapers have devoted much space to the reports of his lectures. An editorial in the *Detroit Evening News* says—Most people will be inclined to think that Swami Vivekananda did better last night in his opera-house lecture than he did in any of his former lectures in this city. The merit of the Hindu's utterances last night lay in their clearness. He drew a very sharp line of distinction between Christianity and Christianity, and told his audience plainly wherein he himself is a Christian in one sense and not a Christian in another sense. He also drew a sharp line between Hinduism and Hinduism, carrying the implication that he desired to be classed as a Hindu only in its better sense. Swami Vivekananda stands superior to all criticism when he says—"We want missionaries of Christ. Let such come to India by the hundreds and thousands. Bring Christ's life to us and let it permeate the very core of society. Let Him be preached in every village and corner of India."

When a man is as sound as that on the main question, all else that he may say must refer to the subordinate details. There is infinite humiliation in this spectacle of a pagan priest reading lessons of conduct and of life to the men who have assumed the spiritual supervision of Greenland's icy mountains and India's coral strand; but the sense of humiliation is the *sine qua non* of most reforms in this world. Having said what he did of the glorious life of the author of the Christian faith, Vivekananda has the right to lecture the way he has, the men who profess to represent that life among the nations abroad. And after all, how like the Nazarene that sounds—"Provide neither gold nor silver, nor brass in your purses, nor scrip for your journey, neither two coats, neither shoes, nor yet staves ; for the workman is worthy of his meat." Those who have become at all familiar with the religious literature of India before the advent of Vivekananda, are best prepared to understand the utter abhorrence of the Orientals of our Western commercial spirit—or what Vivekananda calls, "the shopkeeper's spirit"—in all that we do even in our very religion.

Here is a point for the missionaries which they cannot afford to ignore. They who would convert the Eastern world of paganism, must live up to what they preach, in contempt for the kingdoms of this world and all the glory of them.

Brother Vivekananda considers India the most moral nation in the world. Though in bondage, its spirituality still endures. Here are extracts from the notices of some of his recent Detroit addresses :—At this point the lecturer struck the great moral keynote of his discourse stating that with his people it was the belief that all non-self is good and all self is bad. This point was emphasised throughout the evening and might be termed the text of the address. "To build a home is selfish, argues the Hindu, so he builds it for the worship of God and for the entertainment of guests. To cook food is selfish, so he cooks it for the poor; he will serve himself last if any hungry stranger applies, and this feeling extends throughout the length and breadth of the land. Any man can ask for food and shelter and any house will be opened to him."

"The caste system has nothing to do with religion. A man's occupation is hereditary—a carpenter is born a carpenter; a goldsmith a goldsmith; a workman, a workman; and a priest, a priest."

"Two gifts are especially appreciated the gift of learning and the gift of life. But the gift of learning takes precedence. One may save a man's life, and that is excellent; one may impart to another knowledge, and that is better. To instruct for money is an evil, and to do this would bring opprobrium upon the head of the man who barters learning for gold as though it were an article of trade. The Government makes gifts from time to time to the instructors, and the moral effect is better than it would be if the conditions were the same as exist in certain alleged civilised countries." The speaker had asked throughout the length and breadth of the land what was the definition of "civilisation," and he had asked the question in many countries. Sometimes the reply has been, "What we are, that is civilisation." He begged to differ in the definition of the word. A nation may conquer the waves, control the elements, develop the utilitarian problems of life seemingly to the utmost limits, and yet not realise that in the individual, the highest type of civilisation is found in him who has learned to conquer self. This condition is found more in India than in any other country on earth, for there the material conditions are subservient to the spiritual, and the individual looks to the soul manifestations in everything that has life, studying Nature to this end. Hence, that gentle disposition to endure with indomitable patience the flings of what appears unkind fortune, the while there is a full consciousness of a spiritual strength and knowledge greater than that possessed by any other people. Therefore the existence of a country and people from which flows an unending stream, that attracts the attention of thinkers far and near to approach and throw from their shoulders an oppressive earthly burden.

This lecture was prefaced with the statement that the speaker had been asked many questions. A number of these he preferred to answer privately, but three he had selected, for reasons which would appear, to answer from the pulpit. They were,—"Do the people of India throw their children into the jaws of the crocodiles?" "Do they kill themselves beneath the wheels of Jagannath?" "Do they burn widows with their husbands?" The first question the lecturer treated in the same vein, as an American abroad would, in answering enquiries about Indians running round in the streets of New York, and similar myths which are even to-day entertained by many persons on the Continent. The statement was too ludicrous to give a serious response to it. When asked by certain well-meaning but ignorant people why they gave only female children to the crocodiles, he could only ironically reply, that probably it was because they were softer and more tender and could be more easily masticated by the inhabitants of the river in that benighted country. Regarding the Jagannath legend, the lecturer explained the old practice of the Car-festival in the sacred city, and remarked that possibly a few pilgrims in their zeal to grasp the rope and participate in the drawing of the Car, slipped and fell and were so destroyed. Some such mishaps had been exaggerated into the distorted versions from which the good people of other countries shrank with horror. Vivekananda denied that people burned widows. It was true, however, that widows had burned themselves. In the few cases where this had happened, they had been urged not to do so by holy men, who were always opposed to suicide. Where the devoted widows insisted, stating that they desired to accompany their husbands in the transformation that had taken place, they were obliged to submit themselves to the fiery test. That is, they thrust their hands within the flames, and if they permitted them to be consumed, no further opposition was placed in the way of the fulfilment of their desires. But India is not the only country where women who have loved, have followed immediately the loved one to the realms of immortality ; suicide in such cases have occurred in every land. It is an uncommon bit of fanaticism in any country ; as unusual in India as elsewhere. "No," the speaker repeated, "the people do not burn women in India ; nor have they ever burned witches."

This latter touch is decidedly acute by way of reflection. No analysis of the philosophy of the Hindu Monk need be attempted here, except to say that it is based in general on the struggle of the soul to individually attain

Infinity. One learned Hindu opened the Lowell Institute Course this year. What Mr. Mozoomdar began, might worthily be ended by Brother Vivekananda. This new visitor has by far the most interesting personality, although in the Hindu philosophy, of course, personality is not to be taken into consideration. At the Parliament of Religions, they used to keep Vivekananda until the end of the programme, to make people stay until the end of the session. On a warm day, when a prosy speaker talked too long and people began going home by hundreds, the Chairman would get up and announce that Swami Vivekananda would make a short address just before the benediction. Then he would have the peaceable hundreds perfectly in tether. The four thousand fanning people in the Hall of Columbus would sit smiling and expectant, waiting for an hour or two of other men's speeches, to listen to Vivekananda for fifteen minutes. The Chairman knew the old rule of keeping the best until the last.

OUR DUTY TO THE MASSES[1]

Sri Narayana bless you and yours. Through your Highness' kind help it has been possible for me to come to this country. Since then I have become well known here, and the hospitable people of this country have supplied all my wants. It is a wonderful country and this is a wonderful nation in many respects. No other nation applies so much machinery in their everyday work as do the people of this country. Everything is machine. Then again, they are only one-twentieth of the whole population of the world. Yet they have fully one-sixth of all the wealth of the world. There is no limit to their wealth and luxuries. Yet everything here is so dear. The wages of labour are the highest in the world ; yet the fight between labour and capital is constant.

Nowhere on earth have women so many privileges as in America. They are slowly taking everything into their hands and, strange

[1] Written from Chicago to H. H. the Maharaja of Mysore, on June 23, 1894.

to say, the number of cultured women is much greater than that of cultured men. Of course, the higher geniuses are mostly from the rank of males. With all the criticism of the Westerners against our caste, they have a worse one—that of money. The almighty dollar, as the Americans say, can do anything here.

No country on earth has so many laws, and in no country are they so little regarded. On the whole our poor Hindu people are infinitely more moral than any of the Westerners. In religion they practise here either hypocrisy or fanaticism. Sober-minded men have become disgusted with their superstitious religions and are looking forward to India for new light. Your Highness cannot realise without seeing, how eagerly they take in any little bit of the grand thoughts of the holy Vedas, which resist and are unharmed by the terrible onslaughts of modern science. The theories of creation out of nothing, of a created soul, and of the big tyrant of a God sitting on a throne in a place called heaven, and of the eternal hell-fires, have disgusted all the educated ; and the noble thoughts of the Vedas about the eternity of creation and of the soul, and about the God in our own soul, they are imbibing fast in one shape or other. Within fifty years the educated of the world will come to believe in the eternity of both soul and creation, and in God as our highest and perfect nature, as taught in our holy Vedas. Even now their learned priests are interpreting the Bible in that way. My conclusion is, that they require more spiritual civilisation, and we, more material.

The one thing that is at the root of all evils in India is the condition of the poor. The poor in the West are devils ; compared to them ours are angels, and it is therefore so much the easier to raise our poor. The only service to be done for our lower classes is, to give them education, *to develop their lost individuality.* That is the great task between our people and princes. Up to now nothing has been done in that direction. Priest-power and foreign conquest have trodden them down for centuries, and at last the poor of India have forgotten that they are human beings. They are to be given ideas ; their eyes are to be opened to what is going on in the world around them, and then they will work out their own salvation. Every nation, every man and every woman must work out their own salvation. Give them ideas—that is the only help they require, and then the rest must follow as the effect. Ours is to put the chemicals together, the crystallisation comes in the law of nature. Our duty is to put ideas into their heads, they will do the rest. This is what is to be done in India. It is this idea that has been in my mind for a long time. I could not accomplish it in India, and that was the reason of my coming to this country. The great difficulty in the way of educating the poor, is this. Supposing even your Highness opens a free school in every village, still it would do no good, for the poverty in India is such, that the poor boys would rather go to help their fathers in the fields, or otherwise try to make a living, than come to the school. Now if the mountain does not come to Mahomet, Mahomet must go to the mountain. If the poor boy cannot come to education, education must go to him. There are thousands of single-minded, self-sacrificing Sannyasins in our own country, going from village to village, teaching religion. If some of them can be organised as teachers of secular things also, they will go from place to place, from door to door, not only preaching but teaching also. Suppose two of these men go to a village in the evening with a camera, a globe, some maps, etc. They can teach a great deal of astronomy and geography to the ignorant. By telling stories about different nations, they can give the poor a hundred times more information through the ear than they can get in a lifetime through books. This requires an organisation, which again means money. Men enough there are in India to work out this plan, but alas! they have no money. It is very difficult to set a wheel in motion, but when once set, it goes on with increasing velocity. After seeking help in my own country and failing to get any sympathy from the rich, I came over to this country through your Highness' aid. The Americans do not care a bit whether the poor of India die or live. And why should they, when our own people never think of anything but their own selfish ends?

My noble Prince, this life is short, the vanities of the world are transient, but they alone live who live for others, the rest are more dead than alive. One such high, noble-minded and royal son of India as your Highness, can do much towards raising India on her feet again, and thus leave a name to posterity which shall be worshipped.

That the Lord may make your noble heart feel intensely for the suffering millions of India sunk in ignorance, is the prayer of—

VIVEKANANDA.

REPLY TO THE CALCUTTA ADDRESS[1]

I am in receipt of the resolutions that were passed at the recent Town Hall meeting in Calcutta, and the kind words my fellow-citizens sent over to me.

Accept, sir, my most heartfelt gratitude for your appreciation of my insignificant services.

I am thoroughly convinced that no individual or nation can live by holding itself apart from the community of others, and whenever such an attempt has been made under false ideas of greatness, policy or holiness—the result has always been disastrous to the secluding one.

To my mind, the one great cause of the downfall and the degeneration of India was the building of a wall of custom—whose foundation was hatred of others—round the nation, and the real aim of which in ancient times was to prevent the Hindus

[1] Written from New York on Nov. 18th, 1894, to the President of the public meeting held at the Calcutta Town Hall in appreciation of the Swami's work in the West.

from coming in contact with the surrounding Buddhistic nations.

Whatever cloak ancient or modern sophistry may try to throw over it, the inevitable result—the vindication of the moral law, that none can hate others without degenerating himself—is that the race that was foremost amongst the ancient races is now a by-word, and a scorn among nations. We are object-lessons of the violation of that law which our ancestors were the first to discover and discriminate.

Give and take is the law, and if India wants to raise herself once more, it is absolutely necessary that she brings out her treasures and throws them broadcast among the nations of the earth, and in return be ready to receive what others have to give her. Expansion is life, contraction is death. Love is life and hatred is death. We commenced to die the day we began to hate other races, and nothing can prevent our death unless we come back to expansion, which is life.

We must mix, therefore, with all the races of the earth. And every Hindu that goes out to travel in foreign parts, renders more benefit to his country than hundreds of men who are bundles of superstitions and selfishness, and whose one aim in life seems to be like that of the dog in the manger. The wonderful structures of national life which the Western nations have raised, are supported by the strong pillars of character, and until we can produce numbers of such, it is useless to fret and fume against this or that power.

Do any deserve liberty who are not ready to give it to others? Let us calmly and in a manly fashion go to work, instead of dissipating our energy in unnecessary frettings and fumings. I, for one, thoroughly believe that no power in the universe can withhold from anyone anything he really deserves. The past was great no doubt, but I sincerely believe that the future will be more glorious still.

May Shankara keep us steady in purity, patience and perseverance!

TO MY BRAVE BOYS[1]

Push on with the organisation. Nothing else is necessary but these—*Love, Sincerity* and *Patience.* What is life but growth, i.e. expansion, i.e. *love* ? Therefore all love is life, it is the only law of life, all selfishness is *death,* and this is true here or hereafter. It is life to do good, it is death not to do good to others. Ninety per cent of human brutes you see are dead, are *ghosts*—for none lives, my boys, but he who loves. Feel, my children, feel ; feel for the poor, the ignorant, the downtrodden, feel till the heart stops and the brain reels and you think you will go mad—then pour the soul out at the feet of the Lord and then will come power, help, and indomitable energy. Struggle, struggle was my motto for the last ten years. Struggle, still say I. When it was all dark I used to say, struggle ; when light is breaking in, I still say, struggle. Be not afraid, my children. Look not up in that attitude of fear towards that infinite starry

[1] Written from New York on 19th November, 1894.

vault as if it would crush you. Wait! In a few hours more the whole of it will be under your feet. Wait, money does not pay, nor name; fame does not pay, nor learning. It is love that pays; it is character that cleaves its way through adamantine walls of difficulties.

Now the question before us is this. There cannot be any growth without *liberty*. Our ancestors freed religious thought and we have a wonderful religion, but they put a heavy chain on the feet of society, and our society is, in a word, *horrid, diabolical*. In the West, society always had freedom, and look at them. On the other hand, look at their religion.

Liberty is the first condition of growth. Just as man must have liberty to think and speak, so he must have liberty in food, dress and marriage and in every other thing, so long as he does not injure others.

We talk foolishly against material civilisation. The grapes are sour. Even taking all that foolishness for granted, in all India there are, say, a hundred thousand really spiritual men and women. Now, for the spiritualisation of these, must three hundred millions be sunk in savagery and starvation ? Why should any starve ? How was it possible for the Hindus to have been conquered by the Mohammedans? It was due to the Hindus' ignorance of material civilisation. Even the Mohammedans taught them to wear tailor-made clothes. Would the Hindus have learned from the Mohammedans how to eat in a cleanly way without mixing their food with the dust of the streets ! Material civilisation, nay even luxury, is necessary to create work for the poor. Bread ! Bread ! I do not believe in a God who cannot give me bread here, giving me eternal bliss in heaven ! Pooh ! India is to be raised, the poor are to be fed, education is to be spread, and the evil of priestcraft is to be removed. No priestcraft, no social tyranny ! More bread, more opportunity for everybody ! . . . .

None deserves liberty who is not ready to give liberty. Suppose the English give over to you all the power. Why, the powers that be then, will hold the people down, and let them not have it. Slaves want power to make slaves.

Now, this is to be brought about slowly and by only insisting on our religion, and giving liberty to society. Root up priestcraft from the old religion and you get the best religion in the world. Do you understand me? Can you make a European society with India's religion? I believe it is possible and must be.

The grand plan is to start a colony in Central India, where you can follow your own ideas independently, and then a little leaven will leaven all. In the meanwhile form a Central Association, and go on branching off all over India. Start only on religious grounds now, and do not preach any violent social reform at present; only do not countenance foolish superstitions. Try to revive society on the old grounds of universal salvation and equality as laid down by the old Masters, such as Shankaracharya, Ramanuja and Chaitanya.

Have fire and spread all over. Work, work. Be the servant while leading, be unselfish, and *never listen to one friend in private accusing another.* Have infinite patience and success is yours.

Now take care of this: Do not try to "boss" others, as the Yankees say. Because I always direct my letters to you, you need not try to show your consequence over my other friends. I know you never can be such a fool, but still I think it my duty to warn you. This is what kills all organisations. Work, work, for, to work only for the good of others is life.

I want that there should be no hypocrisy, no Jesuitism, no roguery. I have depended always on the Lord, always on Truth broad as the light of day. 'Let me not die with stains on my conscience for having played Jesuitism to get up name or fame, or even to do good. There should not be a breath of immorality, nor a stain of policy which is bad.

No shilly-shally, no *esoteric blackguardism,* no secret humbug, nothing should be done in a corner. No special favouritism of the Master, no Master at that even. Onward, my brave boys—money or no money—men or no men! Have you love? Have you God? Onward, and forward to the breach, you are irresistible! . . .

Take care! Beware of everything that is untrue; stick to truth and we shall succeed, may be slowly but surely. Work on as if I never existed. Work as if on each of you depended the whole work. Fifty centuries are looking on you, the future of India depends on you. Work on. I do not know when I shall be able to come. This is a great field for work. They can at best praise in India, but they will not give a cent for anything; and where shall they get it, *beggars* themselves? Then, they have lost the faculty of doing public good for the last two thousand years or more. They are just learning the ideas of nation, public, etc. So I need not blame them.

Blessings to you all!

A PLAN OF WORK FOR INDIA[1]

It is with a heart full of love, gratitude and trust, that I take up my pen to write to you. Let me tell you first, that you are one of the few men that I have met in my life, who are thorough in their convictions. You have a whole-souled possession of a wonderful combination of feeling and knowledge, and withal a practical ability to bring ideas into realised forms. Above all, you are sincere, and as such I confide to you some of my ideas.

The work has begun well in India, and it should not only be kept up but pushed on with the greatest vigour. Now or never is the time. After taking a far and wide view of things, my mind has now been concentrated on the following plan. First, it would be well to open a Theological College in Madras, and then gradually extend its scope ; to give a thorough

1 Written to a distinguished Indian from Chicago, 3rd Jan., 1895.

education to young men in the Vedas and the different Bhashyas and Philosophies, including a knowledge of the other religions of the world. At the same time a paper in English and the vernacular should be started as an organ of the College.

This is the first step to be taken, and huge things grow out of small undertakings. Madras just now is following the golden mean by appreciating both the ancient and modern phases of life.

I fully agree with the educated classes in India, that a thorough overhauling of society is necessary. But how to do it ? The destructive plans of Reformers have failed. My plan is this. We have not done *badly* in the past ; certainly not. Our society is not *bad* but good, only I want it to be better still. Not from error to truth, nor from bad to good, but from truth to higher truth, from good to better, best. I tell my countrymen that so far they have done well—now is the time to do better.

Now take the case of caste. In Sanskrit, Jati i.e., species,—now, this is the first idea of creation. Variation (Vichitrata), that is to say Jati, means creation. "I am One, I become many" (various Vedas). Unity is before creation, diversity is creation. Now if this diversity stops, creation will be destroyed. So long as any species is vigorous and active it must throw out varieties. When it ceases or is stopped from breeding varieties, it dies. Now the original idea of Jati was this freedom of the individual to express his nature, his Prakriti, his Jati, his caste, and so it remained for thousands of years. Not even in the latest books is inter-dining prohibited ; nor in any of the older books is inter-marriage forbidden. Then what was the cause of India's downfall ?—the giving up of this idea of caste. As Gita says, with the extinction of caste the world will be destroyed. Now does it seem true that with the stoppage of these variations the world will be destroyed. The present caste is not the real Jati, but a hindrance to its progress. It really has prevented the free action of Jati, i.e., caste or variation. Any crystallised custom or privilege or hereditary class in any shape really prevents caste (Jati) from having its full sway, and whenever any nation ceases to produce this immense variety, it must die. Therefore what I have to tell you, my countrymen, is this: That India fell because you prevented and abolished caste. Every frozen aristocracy or privileged class is a blow to caste and is not-caste. Let Jati have its sway; break down every barrier in the way of caste and we shall rise. Now look at Europe. When it succeeded in giving free scope to caste and took away most of the barriers that stood in the way of individuals each developing his caste—Europe rose. In America, there is the best scope for caste (real Jati) to develop, and so the people are great. Every Hindu knows that Astrologers try to fix the caste of every boy or girl as soon as he or she is born. That is the real caste—the individuality, and Jyotish recognises that. And we can only rise by giving it full sway again. This variety does not mean inequality, nor any special privilege.

This is my method—to show the Hindus that they have to give up nothing, but only to move on in the line laid down by the sages and shake off their inertia, the result of centuries of servitude. Of course, we had to stop advancing during the Mohammedan tyranny, for then it was not a question of progress but of life and death. Now that that pressure has gone, we must move forward, not on the lines of destruction directed by renegades and missionaries, but along our own line—our own road. Everything is hideous because the building is unfinished. We had to stop building during centuries of oppression. Now finish the building and everything will look beautiful in its own place. This is all my plan. I am thoroughly convinced of this. Each nation has a main current in life ; in India it is religion. Make it strong and the waters on either side must move along with it. This is one phase of my line of thought. In time, I hope to bring them all out, but at present I find I have a mission in this country, also. Moreover, I expect help in this country and from here alone. But up to date I could not do anything except spreading my ideas. Now I want that a similar attempt be made in India.

I do not know when I shall go over to India. I obey the leading of the Lord. I am in His hands.

" In this world in search of wealth, Thou art, O Lord, the greatest jewel I have found. I sacrifice myself unto Thee."

" In search of some one to love, Thou art the One Beloved I have found. I sacrifice myself unto Thee." (Yajur Veda Samhita).

May the Lord bless you for ever and ever !

THE PROBLEM OF MODERN INDIA AND ITS SOLUTION[1]

The ancient history of India is full of descriptions of the gigantic energies and their multifarious workings, the boundless spirit, the combination of indomitable action and reaction of the various forces, and above all, the profound thoughtfulness of a godly race. If the word history is understood to mean merely narratives of kings and emperors, and pictures of society—tyrannised over from time to time by the evil passions, haughtiness, avarice, etc., of the rulers of the time, portraying the acts resulting from their good or evil propensities, and how these reacted upon the society of that time—such a history India perhaps does not possess. But every line of that mass of the religious literature of India, her ocean of poetry, her philosophies and various scienti-

[1] The above is a translation of the first Bengali article written by Swami Vivekananda as an introduction to the *Udbodhana,* when it was started on the 14th of January, 1899, as the Bengali fortnightly (afterwards monthly) journal of the Ramakrishna Mission.

fic works are revealing to us—a thousand times more clearly than the narratives of the life-incidents and genealogies of particular kings and emperors can ever do—the exact position and every step made in advance by that vast body of men who, even from before the dawn of civilisation—impelled by hunger and thirst, lust and greed, etc., attracted by the charm of beauty, endowed with a great and indomitable mental power, and moved by various sentiments—arrived through various ways and means at that stage of eminence. Although the heaps of those triumphal flags which they gathered in their innumerable victories over Nature with which they had been waging war for ages have, of late, been torn and tattered by the violent winds of adverse circumstances, and become worn out through age, yet, they still proclaim the glory of Ancient India.

Whether this race slowly proceeded from Central Asia, Northern Europe, or the Arctic regions, and gradually came down and sanctified India by settling there at last or whether the holy land of India was their original native place—we have no proper means of knowing now. Or whether a vast race living in or outside India, being displaced from its original abode, in conformity with natural laws, came in the course of time, to colonise and settle over Europe and other places ;—and whether these people were white or black, blue-eyed or dark-eyed, golden-haired or black-haired ;—all these matters, there is no sufficient ground to prove now, with the one exception of the fact of the kinship of Sanskrit with a few European languages. Similarly, it is not easy to arrive at a final conclusion as to the modern Indians, whether they all are the pure descendants of that race, or how much of the blood of that race is flowing in their veins, or again, what races amongst them have any of that even in them.

However, we do not, in fact, lose much by this uncertainty.

But there is one fact to remember. Of that ancient Indian race, upon which the rays of civilisation first dawned, where deep thoughtfulness first revealed itself, in full glory, there are still found hundreds of thousands of its children, born of its mind—the inheritors of its thoughts and sentiments—ready to claim them.

Crossing over mountains, rivers and oceans, setting at naught, as it were, the obstacles of the distance of space and time, the blood of Indian thought has flowed, and is still flowing into the veins of other nations of the globe, whether in a distinct, or in some subtle unknown way. Perhaps to us belongs the major portion of that universal ancient inheritance.

In a small country lying in the eastern corner of the Mediterranean Sea, beautified and adorned by Nature, and garlanded by well-formed and beautiful-looking islands, lived a race of men—who were few in number, but of a very charming aspect, perfectly formed, and strong in muscles and sinews, light of body, yet possessing steadiness and perseverance ;—and who were unrivalled for the creation of all earthly beauties, as well as endowed with extraordinary practicality and intellect. The other ancient nations used to call them Yavanas, but they called themselves Greeks.

This handful of a vigorous and wonderful race is a unique example in the annals of man. Wherever, and in whatever Nation, there has been, or is, any advance made in earthly science, up to the present day—such as, social, martial, political, sculptural, etc.—there the shadow of ancient Greece has fallen. Let us leave apart the consideration of ancient times, for, even in this modern age, we, the Bengalees, think ourselves proud and enlightened simply by following the footmarks of these Yavana Gurus for these last fifty years, illumining our homes with what light of theirs is reaching us through the European literature.

The whole of Europe nowadays is, in every respect, the disciple of ancient Greece, and her proper inheritor ; so much so, that a wise man of England has said, "Whatever Nature has not created, that is the creation of the Greek mind."

These two gigantic rivers (Aryans and Yavanas) issuing from far-away and different mountains (India and Greece), occasionally come in contact with each other, and whenever such confluence takes place, a tremendous intellectual or spiritual tide, rising in human societies, greatly expands the range of civilisation and confirms the bond of universal brotherhood among men.

Once in far remote antiquity, the Indian philosophy coming in contact with Greek energy, led to the rise of the Persian, the Roman and other great nations. After the invasion of Alexander the Great, these two great waterfalls colliding with each other, deluged nearly half of the globe with spiritual tides, such as Christianity, etc. Again, a similar commingling, resulting in the improvement and prosperity of Arabia, laid the foundation of modern European civilisation. And perhaps, in our own day, such a time for the conjunction of these two gigantic forces has presented itself again. This time their centre is India.

The air of India pre-eminently conduces to quietness ; the nature of the Yavana is the constant expression of power ; profound meditation characterises the one ; the indomitable spirit of dexterous activity, the other: one's motto is "Renunciation", the other's "enjoyment." One's whole energy is directed inwards, the other's outwards; one's whole learning consists in the knowledge of the Self or the Subject, the other's, in the knowledge of the not-Self or the object (perishable creation); one loves Moksha (spiritual freedom), the other loves political independence; one is unmindful of gaining prosperity in this world, the other sets his whole heart on making a heaven of this world; one, aspiring after eternal bliss, is indifferent to all the ephemeral pleasures of this life, and the other, doubting the existence of eternal bliss, or knowing it to be far away, directs his whole energy to the attainment of earthly pleasures as much as possible.

In this age, both these types of mankind are extinct, only their physical and mental children, their works and thoughts are existing.

Europe and America are the advanced children of the Yavanas, a glory to their forefathers; but the modern inhabitants of the land of Bharata are not the glory of the ancient Aryans.

But, as fire remains intact under cover of ashes, so the ancestral fire still remains latent in these modern Indians. Through the grace of the Almighty Power, it is sure to manifest itself in time.

What will accrue when that ancestral fire manifests itself ?

Would the sky of India again appear clouded over by waving masses of smoke springing from the Vedic sacrificial fire ? Or is the glory of Rantideva again going to be revived in the blood of the sacrificed animals ? Are the old customs of Gomedha, Ashvamedha, or perpetuating the lineage from a husband's brother, and other usages of a like nature, to come back again ? Or is the deluge of a Buddhistic propaganda again going to turn the whole of India into a big monastery ? Are the laws of Manu going to be rehabilitated as of yore ? Or, is the discrimination of food, prescribed and forbidden, varying in accordance with geographical dimensions, as it is at the present day, alone going to have its all-powerfull domination over the length and breadth of the country ? Is the caste system to remain, and is it going to depend eternally upon the birthright of a man, or is it going to be determined by his qualification ? And again in that caste system—is the discrimination of food, its touchableness or untouchableness, dependent upon the purity or the impurity of the man who touches it, to be observed as it is in Bengal, or will it assume a form more strict as it does in Madras ? Or, as in the Punjab, will all such restrictions be obliterated ? Are the marriages of the different Varnas to take place from the upper to the lower Varna in the successive order, as in Manu's days, and as it is still in vogue in Nepal ? Or, as in Bengal and other places, are they to be kept restricted to a very limited number of individuals constituting one of the several communities of a certain class of the Varna ? To give a conclusive answer to all these questions is extremely difficult. They become the more difficult of solution, considering the difference in the customs prevailing in different parts of the country—nay, as we find even in the same part of the country such a wide divergence of customs among different castes and families.

Then what is to be ?

What we should have is, what we have not, perhaps what our forefathers even had not ; —that which the Yavanas had ; that, impelled by the life-vibration of which, is issuing forth in rapid succession from the great dynamo of Europe the electric flow of that tremendous power, vivifying the whole world. We want that. We want that energy, that love of independence, that spirit of self-reliance, that immovable fortitude, that dexterity in action, that bond of unity of purpose, that thirst for improvement. Checking a little the constant looking back to the past, we want that expansive vision infinitely projected forward ; and we want—that intense spirit of activity (Rajas) which will flow through our every vein, from head to foot.

What can be a greater giver of peace than "renunciation" ? A little ephemeral worldly good is nothing in comparison with eternal good ; no doubt of that. What can bring greater strength than Sattva Guna (absolute purity of mind) ? It is indeed true that all other kinds of knowledge, are but "non-knowledge" in comparison with Self-knowledge, but I ask—how many are there in the world, fortunate enough to gain that Sattva Guna ? How many in this land of Bharata ? How many have that noble heroism, which can renounce all, shaking off the idea of "I and mine" ? How many are blessed enough to possess that far-sight of wisdom, which makes earthly pleasures appear to be but vanity of vanities ? Where is that broad-hearted man who is apt to forget even his own body in meditating over the beauty and glory of the Divine ? Those who are such are but a handful in comparison to the population of the whole of India ; and in order that these men may attain to their salvation, will the millions and millions of men and women of India have to be crushed under the wheel of the present-day society and religion ?

And what good can come out of such crushing ?

Do you not see—taking up this plea of Sattva, the country has been slowly and slowly drowned in the ocean of Tamas, or dark ignorance ? Where the most dull want to hide their stupidity by covering it with a false desire for the Highest Knowledge, which is beyond all activities, either physical or mental ; where one, born and bred in lifelong laziness, wants to throw the veil of renunciation over his own unfitness for work ; where the most diabolical try to make their cruelty appear under the cloak of austerity, as a part of religion ; where no one has an eye upon his own incapacity, but everyone is ready to lay the whole blame on others ; where knowledge consists only in getting some books by heart, genius consists in chewing the cud of others' thoughts, and the highest glory consists in taking the name of ancestors : do we require any other proof to show that that country is being day by day drowned in utter Tamas ?

Therefore, Sattva, or absolute purity, is now

far away from us. Those amongst us who are not yet fit, but who hope to be fit, to reach to that absolutely pure Paramahamsa state—for them, the acquirement of Rajas, or intense activity, is what is most beneficial now. Unless a man passes through Rajas, can he ever attain to that perfect Sattvika state ? How can one expect Yoga, or union with God, unless one has previously finished with his thirst for Bhoga or enjoyment ? How can renunciation come where there is no Vairagyam or dispassion for all the charms of enjoyment ?

On the other hand, the quality of Rajas is apt to die down as soon as it comes up, like a fire of palm leaves. The presence of Sattva and the Nitya or Eternal Reality, is almost in a state of juxtaposition—Sattva is nearly Nitya. Whereas, the nation in which the quality of Rajas predominates is not so long-lived, but a nation with a preponderance of Sattva is, as it were, immortal. History is a witness to this fact.

In India, the quality of Rajas is almost absent ; the same is the case with Sattva in the

West. It is certain, therefore, that the real life of the Western world depends upon the influx, from India, of the current of Sattva or transcendentalism ; and it is also certain that unless we overpower and submerge our Tamas by the opposite tide of Rajas, we shall never gain any worldly good or welfare in this life ; and it is also equally certain that we shall meet many formidable obstacles in the path of realisation of those noble aspirations and ideals connected with our after-life.

The one end and aim of the *Udbodhana* is to help the union and intermingling of these two forces, as far as it lies in its power.

True, in so doing there is a great danger—lest by this huge wave of Western spirit, are washed away all our most precious jewels, earned through ages of hard labour ; true, there is fear lest falling into its strong whirlpool, even the land of Bharata forgets itself so far as to be turned into a battle-field in the struggle after earthly enjoyments ;—aye, there is fear too, lest going to imitate the impossible and impracticable foreign ways, rooting out as they do our national customs and ideals—we lose all that we hold dear in this life and be undone in the next !

To avoid these calamities we must always keep the wealth of our own home before our eyes, so that every one down to the masses may always know and see what his own ancestral property is—we must exert ourselves to do that and side by side, we should be brave to open our doors to receive all available light from outside. Let rays of light come in, in sharp-driving showers from the four quarters of the earth ; let the intense flood of light flow in from the West—what of that ? Whatever is weak and corrupt is liable to die—what are we to do with it ? If it goes, let it go, what harm does it do to us ? What is strong and invigorating, is immortal ; who can destroy that ?

How many gushing springs and roaring cataracts, how many icy rivulets and ever-flowing streamlets, issuing from the eternal snow-capped peaks of the Himalayas, combine and flow together to form the gigantic river of the gods, the Ganges, and rush impetuously towards the ocean! So, what a variety of thoughts and ideas, how many currents of forces, issuing from innumerable saintly hearts, and from brains of geniuses of various lands have already enveloped India, the land of Karma, the arena for the display of higher human activities! Look! how under the dominion of the English, in these days of electricity, railroad and steamboat, various sentiments, manners, customs and morals are spreading all over the land with lightning speed. Nectar is coming, and along with it, also poison; good is coming, as well as evil. There has been enough of angry opposition and bloodshed; the power of stemming this tide is not in Hindu society. Everything, from water filtered by machinery and drawn from hydrants, down to sugar purified with bone-ash, is being quietly and freely taken by almost every one, in spite of much show of verbal protest. Slowly and slowly, by the strong dint of law, many of our most cherished customs are day by day falling off;—we have no power to withstand that. And why is there no power ? Is truth really powerless ? "Truth alone conquers and not falsehood."—Is this Divine Vedic saying false ? Or who knows but that those very customs which are being swept away by the deluge of the power of Western sovereignty or of Western education, were not real Acharas ; but were Anacharas, after all. This also is a matter for serious consideration.

बहुजनहिताय बहुजनसुखाय—"For the good of the many, as well as for the happiness of the many," in an unselfish manner, with a heart filled with love and reverence, the *Udbodhana* invites all wise and large-hearted men who love their motherland, to discuss these points, and solve these problems ; and being devoid of the feeling of hatred or antagonism, as well as turning itself away from the infliction of abusive language directed towards any individual, or society, or any sect, it offers its whole self for the service of all classes.

To work we have the right, the result is in the hands of the Lord. We only pray—"O

Thou Eternal Spirit, make us spiritual; O Thou Eternal Strength, make us strong; O Thou Mighty One, make us mighty."

THE EDUCATION THAT INDIA NEEDS[1]

In reply to your question about the method of work, the most important thing I have to say is that the work should be started on a scale which would be commensurate with the results desired. I have heard much of your liberal mind, patriotism and steady perseverance from my friend Miss Muller, and the proof of your erudition is evident. I look upon it as great good fortune that you are desirous to know what little this insignificant life has been able to attempt ; I shall state it to you here, as far as I can. But first I shall lay before you my mature convictions for your deliberation.

We have been slaves for ever, i.e., it has never been given to the masses of India to express the inner light which is their inheritance. The Occident has been rapidly advancing towards freedom for the last few centuries. In India,

[1] From a letter written to Srimati Sarala Ghosal, B.A., from Darjeeling, on 24th April, 1897. Translated from Bengali.

it was the king who used to prescribe everything, from Kulinism down to what one should eat and what one should not. In Western countries, the people do everything themselves.

The king now has nothing to say in any social matter ; on the other hand, the Indian people have not yet even the least faith in themselves, what to say of self-reliance. The faith in one's own self, which is the basis of Vedanta, has not yet been even slightly carried into practice. It is for this reason that the Western method—i.e., first of all, discussion about the wished-for end, then the carrying it out by the combination of all the forces—is of no avail even now in this country ; it is for this reason that we appear so greatly conservative under foreign rule. If this be true, then it is a vain attempt to do any great work by means of public discussion. "There is no chance of a headache where there is no head,"—where is the public ? Besides, we are so devoid of strength that our whole energy is exhausted if we undertake to discuss anything ; none is left for work. It is for this reason, I suppose, we observe in Bengal almost always—"Much cry but little wool." Secondly, as I have written before, I do not expect anything from the rich people of India. It is best to work among the youth in whom lies our hope—patiently, steadily and without noise.

Now about work. From the day when education and culture etc. began to spread gradually from patricians to plebeians, grew the distinction between the modern civilisation as of Western countries, and the ancient civilisation as of India, Egypt, Rome, etc. I see it before my eyes, a nation is advanced in proportion as education and intelligence spread among the masses. The chief cause of India's ruin has been the monopolising of the whole education and intelligence of the land, by dint of pride and royal authority, among a handful of men. If we are to rise again, we shall have to do it in the same way, i.e., by spreading education among the masses. A great fuss has been made for half a century about social reform. Travelling through various places of India these last ten years, I observed the country full of social reform associations. But I did not find one association for them, by sucking whose blood the people known as "gentlemen," have become and continue to be gentlemen! How many sepoys were brought by the Mussulmans? How many Englishmen are there? Where except in India can be had millions of men who will cut the throats of their own fathers and brothers for six rupees? Sixty millions of Mussulmans in seven hundred years of Mohammedan rule, and two millions of Christians in one hundred years of Christian rule—what makes it so? Why has originality entirely forsaken the country? Why are our deft-fingered artisans daily becoming extinct, unable to compete with the Europeans? By what power again has the German labourer succeeded in shaking the many-century-grounded firm footing of the English labourer?

Education, education, education alone! Travelling through many cities of Europe and observing in them the comforts and education of even the poor people, there was brought to my mind the state of our own poor people

and I used to shed tears. What made the difference ? Education was the answer I got. Through education, faith in one's own self, and through faith in one's own self the inherent Brahman is waking up in them, while the Brahman in us is gradually becoming dormant. In New York I used to observe the Irish colonists come—downtrodden, haggard-looking, destitute of all possessions at home, penniless and wooden-headed—with their only belongings, a stick and a bundle of rags hanging at the end of it, fright in their steps, alarm in their eyes. A different spectacle in six months—the man walks upright, his attire is changed. In his eyes and steps there is no more sign of fright. What is the cause ? Our Vedanta says that that Irishman was kept surrounded by contempt in his own country—the whole of Nature was telling him with one voice, "Pat, you have no more hope, you are born a slave and will remain so." Having been thus told from his birth, Pat believed in it and hypnotised himself that he was very low, and the Brahman in him shrank away. While no sooner had he landed in America than he heard the shout going up on all sides, "Pat, you are a man as we are, it is man who has done all, a man like you and me can do everything: have courage!" Pat raised his head and saw that it was so, the Brahman within woke up, Nature herself spoke, as it were,—"Arise, awake, and stop not till the goal is reached."

Likewise the education that our boys receive is very negative. The school-boy learns nothing, but has everything of his own broken down—want of Shraddha is the result. The Shraddha which is the keynote of the Veda and the Vedanta—the Shraddha which emboldened Nachiketa to face Yama and question him, through which Shraddha this world moves—the annihilation of that Shraddha! अज्ञश्चाश्रद्दधानश्च संशयात्मा विनश्यति । —"The ignorant, the man devoid of Shraddha, the doubting self runs to ruin." Therefore are we so near destruction. The remedy now is, the spread of education. First of all, Self-knowledge. I do not mean thereby, matted hair, staff, Kamandalu and mountain caves which the word suggests. What do I mean then ? Cannot the knowledge by which is attained even freedom from the bondage of worldly existence, bring ordinary material prosperity ? Certainly it can. Freedom, dispassion, renunciation—all these are the very highest ideals, but स्वल्पमप्यस्य धर्मस्य त्रायते महतो भयात् । "Even a little of this Dharma saves from the great fear (of birth and death)." Dualist, qualified-Monist, Monist, Shaiva, Vaishnava, Shakta, even the Buddhist and the Jain and others—whatever sects have arisen in India are all at one in this respect, that infinite power is latent in this Jivatman (individualised soul); from the ant to the perfect man there is the same Atman in all, the difference being only in manifestation. "As a farmer breaks the obstacles (to the course of water)" (Patanjali's Yoga Sutra, Kaivalyapada, 3). That power manifests as soon as it gets the opportunity and the right place and time. From the highest god to the meanest grass, the same power is present in all—whether manifested or not. We shall have to call forth that power by going from door to door.

Secondly, along with this, education has to be imparted. That is easy to say, but how to reduce it into practice? There are thousands of unselfish, kind-hearted men in our country, who have renounced everything. In the same way as they travel about and give religious instructions without any remuneration, so at least half of them can be trained as teachers, or bearers of such education as we need most. For that, we want first of all a centre in the capital of each Presidency, from whence to spread slowly throughout the whole of India. Two centres have recently been started in Madras and Calcutta, there is hope of more soon. Then, the greater part of the education to the poor should be given orally, time is not yet ripe for schools. Gradually in these main centres will be taught agriculture, industry, etc., and workshops will be established for the furtherance of arts. To sell the manufactures of those workshops in Europe and America, associations will be started like those already in existence. It will be necessary to start centres for women, exactly like those for men. But you are aware how difficult that is in this country. Again, "The snake which bites, must take out its own poison"—and that this is going to be is my firm conviction; the money required for these works would have to come from the West. And for that reason, our religion should be preached in Europe and America. Modern science has undermined the basis of religions like Christianity. Over and above that, luxury is about to kill the religious instinct itself. Europe and America are now looking towards India with expectant eyes—this is the time for philanthropy, this is the time to occupy the hostile strongholds.

In the West, women rule; all influence and power are theirs. If bold and talented women like yourself, versed in Vedanta, go to England to preach, I am sure that every year hundreds of men and women will become blessed by adopting the religion of the land of Bharata. The only woman who went over from our country was Ramabai; her knowledge of

English, Western science and art was limited; still she surprised all. If any one like you go, England will be stirred, what to speak of America! If an Indian woman in Indian dress preach there the religion which fell from the lips of the Rishis of India—I see a prophetic vision—there will rise a great wave which will inundate the whole Western world. Will there be no woman in the land of Maitreyi, Khana, Lilavati, Savitri and Ubhayabharati, who will venture to do this? The Lord knows. England we shall conquer, England we shall possess, through the power of spirituality. नान्यः पन्था विद्यतेऽयनाय —"There is no other way of salvation." Can salvation ever come by getting up meetings and societies? Our conquerors must be made Devas by the power of our spirituality. . . . Conquest of England, Europe and America—this should be our one supreme Mantra at present, in it lies the well-being of the country. Expansion is the sign of life, and we must spread over the world with our spiritual ideals. Alas! this frame is poor, moreover, the physique of a Bengali;

even under this labour a fatal disease has attacked it, but there is the hope,—

उत्पत्स्यतेऽस्ति मम कोऽपि समानधर्मा

कालोह्ययं निरवधिर्विपुला च पृथ्वी ॥

" A kindred spirit is or will be born out of the limitless time and populous earth to accomplish the work."

OUR PRESENT SOCIAL PROBLEMS[1]

स ईश अनिर्वचनीयप्रेमस्वरूपः—"The Lord whose nature is unspeakable love." That this characteristic of God mentioned by Narada is manifest and admitted on all hands is the firm conviction of my life. The aggregate of many individuals is called Samashti (the whole), and each individual is called Vyashti (a part). You and I—each is Vyashti, society is Samashti. You, I, an animal, a bird, a worm, an insect, a tree, a creeper, the earth, a planet, a star—each is Vyashti, while this universe is Samashti, which is called Virat, Hiranyagarbha or Ishvara in Vedanta, and Brahma, Vishnu, Devi, etc., in the Puranas. Whether or not Vyashti has individual freedom, and if it has, what should be its measure, whether or not Vyashti should completely sacrifice its own will, its own happiness for Samashti—are the perennial problems before every society. Society everywhere is busy finding the solution of these problems.

[1] Written to a Bengali lady from Deoghar (Vaidyanath), on 23rd December, 1900. Translated from Bengali.

These, like big waves, are agitating modern Western society. The doctrine which demands the sacrifice of individual freedom to social supremacy is called socialism, while that which advocates the cause of the individual is called individualism.

Our motherland is a glowing example of the results and consequence of the eternal subjection of the individual to society and forced self-sacrifice by dint of institution and discipline. In this country men are born according to Shastric injunctions, they eat and drink by prescribed rules througout life, they go through marriage and kindred functions in the same way; in short, they even die according to Shastric injunctions. This hard discipline, with the exception of one great good point, is fraught with evil. The good point is, that men can do one or two things well, with very little effort, having practised them every day through generations. The delicious rice and curry which a cook of this country prepares with the aid of three lumps of earth and a few sticks can be had nowhere else. With the simple mechanism of an antediluvian loom, worth one rupee, and the feet put in a pit, it is possible to make kincobs worth twenty rupees a yard, in this country alone. A torn mat, an earthen lamp, and that fed by castor oil—with the aid of materials such as these, wonderful *savants* are produced in this country alone. An all-forbearing attachment to an ugly and deformed wife, and a lifelong devotion to a worthless and villainous husband, are possible in this country alone. Thus far the bright side.

But all these things are done by people guided like lifeless machines—there is no mental activity, no unfoldment of the heart, no vibration of life, no flux of hope ; there is no strong stimulation of the will, no experience of keen pleasure, nor the contract of intense sorrow ; there is no stir of inventive genius, no desire for novelty, no appreciation of new things. Clouds never pass away from this mind, the radiant picture of the morning sun never charms this heart. It never even occurs to this mind if there is any better state than this ; where it does, it cannot convince ; in the event of conviction, effort is lacking ; and even where there is effort, lack of enthusiasm kills it out.

If living by rule alone ensures excellence, if it be virtue to strictly follow the rules and customs handed down through generations, say then, who is more virtuous than a tree, who is a greater devotee, a holier saint than a railway train ? Who has ever seen a piece of stone transgress a natural law ? Who has ever known cattle to commit sin ?

The huge steamer, the mighty railway engine—they are non-intelligent, they move, turn, and run, but they are without intelligence. And yonder tiny worm which moved away from the railway line to save its life, why is it intelligent ? There is no manifestation of will in the machine, the machine never wishes to transgress law ; the worm wants to oppose law, rises against law whether it succeeds or not, therefore it is intelligent. Greater is the happiness, higher is the Jiva, in proportion as this will is more successfully manifest. The will of

God is perfectly fruitful, therefore He is the highest.

What is education ? Is it book-learning ? No. Is it diverse knowledge ? Not even that. The training by which the current and expression of will are brought under control and become fruitful, is called education. Now consider, is that education, as a result of which the will being continuously chocked by force through generations, is now well-nigh killed out—under whose sway, why mention new ideas, even the old ones are disappearing one by one—is that education which is slowly making man a machine ? It is more blessed, in my opinion, even to go wrong impelled by one's free will and intelligence than to be good as an automaton. Again, can that be called society which is formed by an aggregate of men who are like lumps of clay, like lifeless machines, like heaped up pebbles ? How can such society fare well ? Were good possible, then instead of being slaves for hundreds of years we would have been the greatest nation on earth, and this soil of India, instead of being a mine of stupidity, would have been the eternal fountain-head of learning.

Is not self-sacrifice, then, a virtue ? Is it not the most virtuous deed to sacrifice the happiness of one, the welfare of one, for the sake of the many ? Exactly, but as the Bengali adage goes, "Can beauty be manufactured by rubbing and scrubbing ? Can love be generated by effort and compulsion ?" What glory is there in the renunciation of an eternal beggar ? What virtue is there in the sense-control of one devoid of sense-power ? What again is the self-sacrifice of one devoid of idea, devoid of heart, devoid of high ambition and devoid of the conception of what constitutes society ? What expression of devotedness to a husband is there by forcing a widow to commit Sati ? Why make people do virtuous deeds by teaching superstitions ? I say, liberate, undo the shackles of people as much as you can. Can dirt be washed by dirt ? Can bondage be removed by bondage ? Where is the instance ? When you would be able to sacrifice all desire for happiness for the sake of society, then you would be the Buddha, then you would be free ; that is far off. Again, do you think the way to it lies through oppression ? "Oh, what examples of self-denial are our widows ! Oh, how sweet is child-marriage ! Is another such custom possible ! Can there be anything but love between husband and wife in such a marriage !"—such is the whine going round nowadays. But as to the men, the masters of the situation, there is no need of self-denial for them ! Is there a virtue higher than serving others ? But the same does not apply to Brahmins—you others do it ! The truth is, that in this country parents and relatives can ruthlessly sacrifice the best interests of their children and others, for their own selfish ends, to save themselves by a compromise to society, and the teaching of generations rendering the mind callous, has made it perfectly easy. He, the brave alone, can deny self. The coward, afraid of the lash, with one hand wipes his eyes and gives with the other. Of what avail are such gifts ? It is a far cry to love universal. The young plant should be hedged in and taken care of. One can hope to gradually attain to universal love, if one can learn to love one object unselfishly. If devotion to one particular Ishtadeva is attained, devotion to the universal Virat is gradually possible.

Therefore, when one has been able to deny self for an individual, one should talk of self-sacrifice for the sake of society, not before. It is action with desire that leads to action without desire. Is the renunciation of desire possible, if desire did not exist in the beginning ? And what could it mean ? Can light have any meaning if there is no darkness ?

Worship with desire, with attachment, comes first. Commence with the worship of the little, then the greater will come of itself.

Mother, be not anxious. It is against the big tree that the great wind strikes. "Poking a fire makes it burn better" ; "A snake struck on the head raises its hood"—and so on : When there comes affliction in the heart, when the storm of sorrow blows all around, and it seems light will be seen no more, when hope and courage are almost gone, it is then, in the midst of this great spiritual tempest, that the light of Brahman within gleams. Brought up in the lap of luxury, lying on a bed of roses and never shedding a tear, who has ever become great, who has even unfolded the Brahman within ? Why do you fear to weep ? Weep ! Weeping clears the eyes and brings about intuition. Then the vision of diversity—man, animal, tree—slowly melting away, makes room for the infinite realisation of Brahman everywhere and in everything. Then,—

समं पश्यन् हि सर्वत्र समवस्थितमीश्वरम् ।
न हिनस्त्यात्मनात्मानं ततो याति परां गतिम् ॥

" Verily, seeing the same God equally existent everywhere, he does not injure the Self by the self, and so goes to the Supreme Goal."

HISTORICAL EVOLUTION OF INDIA

नासतो सत् जायेत !—Existence cannot be produced by non-existence. . . .

Non-existence can never be the cause of what exists. Something cannot come out of nothing. That the law of causation is omnipotent and knows no time or place when it did not exist, is a doctrine as old as the Aryan race, sung by its ancient poet-seers, formulated by its philosophers, and made the corner-stone upon which the Hindu man even of to-day builds his whole scheme of life.

There was an inquisitiveness in the race to start with, which very soon developed into bold analysis, and though in the first attempt the work turned out might be like the attempts with shaky hands of the future master-sculptor, it very soon gave way to strict science, bold attempts and startling results.

Its boldness made these men search every brick of their sacrificial altars ; scan, cement and pulverise every word of their scriptures ; arrange, re-arrange, doubt, deny or explain the ceremonies. It turned their gods inside out, and assigned only a secondary place to their omnipotent, omniscient, omnipresent Creator of the universe, their ancestral Father-in-heaven ; or threw Him altogether overboard as useless, and started a world-religion without Him with even now the largest following of any religion. It evolved the science of geometry from the arrangements of bricks to build various altars and startled the world with astronomical knowledge that arose from the attempts accurately to time their worship and oblations. It made their contribution to the science of mathematics the largest of any race ancient or modern, and their knowledge of chemistry, of metallic compounds in medicine, their scale of musical notes, their invention of the bow-instruments, of great service in the building of modern European civilisation. It led them to invent the science of building up the child mind through shining fables, which every child in every civilised country learns in a nursery or a school and carries an impress of through life.

Behind and before this analytical keenness, covering it as in a velvet sheath, was the other great mental peculiarity of the race—poetic insight. Its religion, its philosophy, its history, its ethics, its politics were all inlaid in a flower-bed of poetic imagery—the miracle of language which was called Sanskrit, or "perfected," lending itself to expressing and manipulating them better than any other tongue. The aid of melodious numbers was invoked even to express the hard facts of mathematics.

This analytical power and the boldness of poetical visions which urged it onward are the two great internal causes in the make-up of the Hindu race. They together formed, as it were, the keynote to the national character. This combination is what is always making the race press onwards beyond the senses—the secret of those speculations which are like the steel blades the artisans used to manufacture—cutting through bars of iron, yet pliable enough to be easily bent into a circle.

They wrought poetry in silver and gold ; the symphony of jewels, the maze of marble wonders, the music of colours, the fine fabrics which belong more to the fairyland of dreams than to the real—have back of them thousands of years of working of this national trait.

Arts and sciences, even the realities of domestic life, are covered with a mass of poetical conceptions, which are pressed forward till the sensuous touches the supersensuous and the real gets the rose-hue of the unreal.

The earliest glimpses we have of this race show it already in the possession of this characteristic, as an instrument of some use in its hands. Many forms of religion and society must have been left behind in the onward march, before we find the race as depicted in the scriptures, the Vedas.

An organised pantheon, elaborate ceremonials, divisions of society into hereditary classes necessitated by a variety of occupations, a great many necessaries and a good many luxuries of life are already there.

Most modern scholars are agreed that surroundings as to climate and conditions purely Indian were not yet working on the race.

Onward through several centuries, we come to a multitude surrounded by snows of the Himalayas on the north and the heat of the south—vast plains, interminable forests, through which mighty rivers roll their tides. We catch a glimpse of different races—Dravidians, Tartars, and Aboriginals pouring in their quota of blood, of speech, of manners and religions—and at last a great nation emerges to our view, still keeping the type of the Aryan ; stronger, broader, and more organised by the assimilation.

We find the central assimilative core giving its type and character to the whole mass, clinging on with great pride to its name of "Aryan," and, though willing to give other races the benefits of its civilisation, it was by no means willing to admit them within the "Aryan" pale.

The Indian climate again gave a higher direction to the genius of the race. In a land where nature was propitious and yielded easy victories, the national mind started to grapple with and conquer the higher problems of life in the field of thought. Naturally the thinker, the priest, became the highest class in the Indian society, and not the man of the sword. The priests again, even at that dawn of history, put most of their energy in elaborating rituals ; and when the nation began to find the load of ceremonies and lifeless rituals too heavy—came the first philosophical speculations, and the royal race was the first to break through the maze of killing rituals.

On the one hand, the majority of the priests impelled by economical considerations were bound to defend that form of religion which made their existence a necessity of society and assigned them the highest place in the scale of caste ; on the other hand, the king-caste, whose strong right hand guarded and guided the nation and who now found itself as leading in the higher thoughts also, were loath to give up the first place to men who only knew how to conduct a ceremonial. There were then others, recruited from both the priests and king-castes, who ridiculed equally the ritualists and philosophers, declared spiritualism as fraud and priestcraft, and upheld the attainment of material comforts as the highest goal of life. The people, tired of ceremonials and wondering at the philosophers, joined in masses the materialists. This was the beginning of that caste question and that triangular fight in India between ceremonials, philosophy and materialism which has come down unsolved to our own days.

The first solution of the difficulty attempted was by applying the eclecticism which from the earliest days had taught the people to see in differences the same truth in various garbs. The great leader of this school, Krishna himself—of royal race—and his sermon, the Gita, have after various vicissitudes brought about by the upheavals of the Jains, the Buddhists and other sects, fairly established themselves as the "Prophet" of India and the truest philosophy of life. Though the tension was toned down for the time, it did not satisfy the social wants which were among the causes—

8

the claim of the king-race to stand first in the scale of caste and the popular intolerance of priestly privilege. Krishna had opened the gates of spiritual knowledge and attainment to all irrespective of sex or caste, but he left undisturbed the same problem on the social side. This again has come down to our own days, in spite of the gigantic struggle of the Buddhists, Vaishnavas, etc., to attain social equality for all.

Modern India admits spiritual equality of all souls—but strictly keeps the social difference.

Thus we find the struggle renewed all along the line in the seventh century before the Christian era and finally in the sixth, overwhelming the ancient order of things under Shakya Muni, the Buddha. In their reaction against the privileged priesthood Buddhists swept off almost every bit of the old ritual of the Vedas, subordinated the gods of the Vedas to the position of servants to their own human saints and declared the "Creator and Supreme Ruler" as an invention of priestcraft and superstition.

But the aim of Buddhism was reform of the Vedic religion by standing against ceremonials requiring offerings of animals, against hereditary caste, exclusive priesthood and against belief in permanent souls. It never attempted to destroy that religion, or overturn the social order. It introduced a vigorous method, by organising a class of Sannyasins into a strong monastic brotherhood, and the Brahmavadinis into a body of nuns—by introducing images of saints in the place of altar-fires.

It is probable that the reformers had for centuries the majority of the Indian people with them. The older forces were never entirely pacified, but they underwent a good deal of modification during the centuries of Buddhistic supremacy.

In ancient India the centres of national life were always the intellectual and spiritual and not political. Of old, as now, political and social power has been always subordinated to spiritual and intellectual. The outburst of national life was round colleges of sages and spiritual teachers. We thus find the Samitis of the Panchalas, of the Kashyas (Benares), the Maithilas standing out as great centres of spiritual culture and philosophy, even in the Upanishads. Again these centres in turn became the focus of political ambition of the various divisions of the Aryans.

The great epic Mahabharata tells us of the war of the Kurus and Panchalas for supremacy over the nation, in which they destroyed each other. The spiritual supremacy veered round and centred in the East among the Magadhas and Maithilas, and after the Kuru-Panchala war a sort of supremacy was obtained by the kings of Magadha.

The Buddhist reformation and its chief field of activity were also in the same eastern region ; and when the Maurya kings, forced possibly by the bar sinister on their escutcheon, patronised and led the new movement, the new priest power joined hands with the political power of the empire of Pataliputra. The popularity of Buddhism and its fresh vigour made the Maurya kings the greatest emperors that India ever had. The power of the Maurya sovereigns made Buddhism that world-wide religion that we see even to-day.

The exclusiveness of the old form of Vedic religions debarred it from taking ready help from outside. At the same time it kept it pure and free from many debasing elements which Buddhism in its propagandist zeal was forced to assimilate.

This extreme adaptability in the long run made Indian Buddhism lose almost all its individuality, and extreme desire to be of the people made it unfit to cope with the intellectual forces of the mother religion in a few centuries. The Vedic party in the meanwhile got rid of a good deal of its most objectionable features, as animal sacrifice, and took lessons from the rival daughter in the judicious use of images, temple processions, and other impressive performances and stood ready to take within her fold the whole empire of Indian Buddhism already tottering to its fall.

And the crash came, with the Scythian invasions and the total destruction of the empire of Pataliputra.

The invaders, already incensed at the invasion of their central Asiatic home by the preachers of Buddhism, found in the sun-worship of the Brahmins a great sympathy with their own solar religion—and when the Brahminist party were ready to adapt and spiritualise many of the customs of the new-comers, the invaders threw themselves heart and soul into the Brahminic cause.

Then there is a veil of darkness and shifting shadows, there are tumults of war, rumours of massacres, and the next scene rises upon a new phase of things.

The empire of Magadha was gone. Most of northern India was under the rule of petty chiefs always at war with one another. Buddhism was almost extinct, except in some eastern and Himalayan provinces and in the extreme south ; and the nation after centuries of struggle against the power of a hereditary priest awoke to find itself in the clutches of a double priesthood of hereditary Brahmins and exclusive monks of the new regime, with all the powers of the Buddhistic organisation and without their sympathy for the people.

A renaiscent India bought by the valour and blood of the heroic Rajputs, defined by the merciless intellect of a Brahmin from the same historical thought-centre of Mithila, led by a new philosophical impulse organised by Shankara and his bands of Sannyasins and beautified by the arts and literature of the courts of Malava—arose on the ruins of the old.

The task before it was profound, problems vaster than any their ancestors had ever faced. A comparatively small and compact race, of the same blood and speech and the same social and religious aspiration, trying to save its unity by unscalable walls around itself, grew huge by multiplication and addition during the Buddhistic supremacy and was divided by race, colour, speech, spiritual instinct and social ambitions into hopelessly jarring factions. And this had to be unified and welded into one gigantic nation. This task Buddhism had also come to solve, and had taken it up when the proportions were not so vast.

So long it was a question of Aryanising the

other types that were pressing for admission and thus out of different elements making a huge Aryan body. In spite of concessions and compromises Buddhism was eminently successful and remained the national religion of India. But the time came when the allurements of sensual forms of worship, indiscriminately taken in along with various low races, were too dangerous for the central Aryan core, and a longer contact would certainly have destroyed the civilisation of the Aryans. Then came a natural reaction for self-preservation, and Buddhism as a separate sect ceased to live in most parts of its land of birth.

The reaction-movement led in close succession by Kumarilla in the north and Shankara and Ramanuja in the south has become the last embodiment of that vast accumulation of sects and doctrines and rituals called Hinduism. For the last thousand years or more, its great task has been assimilation, with now and then an outbrust of reformation. This reaction first wanted to revive the rituals of the Vedas—failing which, it made the Upanishads or the philosophic portions of the Vedas its basis. It brought Vyasa's systems of Mimamsa philosophy and Krishna's sermon, the Gita, to the forefront, and all succeeding movements have followed the same. The movement of Shankara forced its way through its high intellectuality, but it could be of little service to the masses, because of its adherence to strict caste-laws, very small scope for ordinary emotion, and making Sanskrit the only vehicle of communication. Ramanuja, on the other hand, with a most practical philosophy, a great appeal to the emotions, an entire denial of birthrights before spiritual attainments and appeals through the popular tongue, completely succeeded in bringing the masses back to the Vedic religion.

The northern reaction of ritualism was followed by the fitful glory of the Malava empire. With the destruction of that in a short time, northern India went to sleep as it were, for a long period, to be rudely awakened by the thundering onrush of Mohammedan cavalry across the passes of Afghanisthan. In the south, however, the spiritual upheaval of Shankara and Ramanuja was followed by the usual Indian sequence of united races and powerful empires. It was the home of refuge of Indian religion and civilisation, when northern India from sea to sea lay bound at the feet of Central Asiatic conquerors. The Mohammedan tried for centuries to subjugate the south, but can scarcely be said to have got even a strong foothold ; and when the strong and united empire of the Moguls was very near completing its conquest, the hills and plateaus of the south poured in their bands of fighting peasant horsemen, determined to die for the religion which Ramdas preached and Tuka sang, and in a short time the gigantic empire of the Moguls was only a name.

The movements in northern India during the Mohammedan period are characterised by their uniform attempt to hold the masses back from joining the religion of the conquerors—which brought in its train social and spiritual equality for all.

The friars of the orders founded by Rama-

nanda, Kabir, Dadu, Chaitanya or Nanak were all agreed in preaching the equality of man, however differing from each other in philosophy. Their energy was for the most part spent in checking the rapid conquest of Islam among the masses, and they had very little left to give birth to new thoughts and aspirations. Though evidently successful in their purpose of keeping the masses within the folds of the old religion, and tempering the fanaticism of the Mohammedans, they were mere apologists, struggling to obtain permission to live.

One great prophet, however, arose in the north, Govind Singh, the last Guru of the Sikhs, with creative genius, and the result of his spiritual work was followed by the well-known political organisation of the Sikhs. We have seen throughout the history of India, a spiritual upheaval always succeeded by a political unity extending over more or less area of the continent, which in its turn helps to strengthen the spiritual aspiration that brings it to being. But the spiritual aspiration that preceded the rise of the Mahratta or the Sikh empire was entirely reactionary. We seek in vain to find in the court of Poona or Lahore even a ray of reflection of that intellectual glory which surrounded the courts of the Moguls, much less the brilliance of Malava or Vidyanagar. It was intellectually the darkest period of Indian history, and both these meteoric empires, representing the upheaval of mass-fanaticism and hating culture with all their hearts, lost all their motive power as soon as they had succeeded in destroying the rule of the hated Mohammedans.

Then there came again a period of confusion. Friends and foes, the Mogul empire and its destroyers, and the till then peaceful foreign traders, French and English, all joined in a *melee* of fight. For more than half a century there was nothing but war and pillage and destruction, and when the smoke and dust cleared, England was stalking victorious over the rest. There has been half a century of peace, and law and order under the sway of Britain. Time alone will prove if it is the order of progress or not.

There have been a few religious movements amongst the Indian people during the British rule, following the same line that was taken up by northern Indian sects during the sway of the empire of Delhi. They are the voices of the dead or the dying—the feeble tones of a terrorised people, pleading for permission to live. They are ever eager to adjust their spiritual or social surroundings according to the tastes of the conquerors—if they are only left the right to live, especially the sects under the English domination, in which social differences with the conquering race are more glaring than the spiritual. The Hindu sects of the century seem to have set one ideal of truth before them—the approval of their English masters. No wonder that these sects have mushroom lives to live. The vast body of the Indian people religiously hold aloof from them and the only popular recognition they get is the jubilation of the people when they die.

But possibly for some time yet it cannot be otherwise.

MARCH ON[1]

Yesterday, Mrs.—, the lady superintendent of the women's prison, was here. They don't call it prison but reformatory here. It is the grandest thing I have seen in America. How the inmates are benevolently treated, how they are reformed and sent back as useful members of society; how grand, how beautiful, you must see to believe! And, oh, how my heart ached to think of what we think of the poor, the low in India. They have no chance, no escape, no way to climb up. The poor, the low, the sinner in India have no friends, no help—they cannot rise, try however they may. They sink lower and lower every day, they feel the blows showering upon them by a cruel society, and they do not know whence the blow comes. They have forgotten that they too are men. And the result is slavery. Thoughtful people within the last few years have seen it, but unfortunately laid it at the

[1] From a letter written from America on 30th August, 1893.

door of the Hindu religion, and to them the only way of bettering is by crushing this grandest religion of the world. Hear me, my friend, I have discovered the secret through the grace of the Lord. Religion is not at fault. On the other hand, your religion teaches you that every being is only your own self multiplied. But it was the want of practical application, the want of sympathy—the want of heart. The Lord once more came to you as Buddha and taught you how to feel, how to sympathise with the poor, the miserable, the sinner, but you heard him not. Your priests invented the horrible story that the Lord was here for deluding demons with false doctrines! True, indeed, but we are the demons, not those that believed. And just as the Jews denied the Lord Jesus and are since that day wandering over the world as homeless beggars, tyrannised over by everybody, so you are bond-slaves to any nation that thinks it worth while to rule over you. Ah, tyrants! you do not know that the obverse is tyranny and the reverse slavery. The slave and the tyrant are synonymous.

. . . This state of things must be removed, not by destroying religion but by following the great teachings of the Hindu faith, and joining with it the wonderful sympathy of that logical development of Hinduism—Buddhism.

A hundred thousand men and women, fired with the zeal of holiness, fortified with the eternal faith in the Lord, and nerved to lion's courage by their sympathy for the poor and the fallen and the downtrodden, will go over the length and breadth of the land, preaching the gospel of salvation, the gospel of self ; the gospel of social raising-up—the gospel of Equality.

No religion on earth preaches the dignity of humanity in such a lofty strain as Hinduism, and no religion on earth treads upon the necks of the poor and the low in such a fashion as Hinduism. The Lord has shown me that religion is not at fault, but it is the Pharisees and Sadducees in Hinduism, hypocrites, who invent all sorts of engines of tyranny in the shape of doctrines of Paramarthika and Vyavaharika (absolute and relative truth).

Despair not, remember the Lord says in the Gita, "To work you have the right but not to the result." Gird up your loins, my boy. I am called by the Lord for this. I have dragged through a whole life full of crosses and tortures, I have seen the nearest and dearest die, almost of starvation—I have been ridiculed, distrusted, and have suffered for my sympathy for the very men who scoff and scorn. Well, my boy, this is the school of misery, which is also the school for great souls and prophets for the cultivation of sympathy, of patience, and above all, of an indomitable iron-will which quakes not even if the universe be pulverised at our feet. I pity them. It is not their fault. They are children, yea, veritable children, though they be great and high in society. Their eyes see nothing beyond their little horizon of a few yards—the routine work, eating, drinking, earning and begetting, following each other in mathematical precision. They know nothing beyond, happy little souls! Their sleep is never disturbed. Their nice little brownstudies of lives never rudely shocked by the wail of woe, of misery, of degradation and poverty, that has filled the Indian atmosphere—the result of centuries of oppression. They little dream of the ages of tyranny, mental, moral and physical, that has reduced the image of God to a mere beast of burden ; the emblem of the divine Mother, to a slave to bear children ; and life itself, a curse. But there are others who see, feel, and shed tears of blood in their hearts, who think that there is a remedy for it, and who are ready to apply this remedy at any cost, even to the giving up of life. And "Of such is the kingdom of Heaven." Is it not then natural, my friends, that they have no time to look down from their heights to the vagaries of these contemptible little insects, ready every moment to spit their little venoms ?

Trust not to the so-called rich, they are more dead than alive. The hope lies in you—in the meek, the lowly, but the faithful. Have faith in the Lord ; no policy, it is nothing. Feel for the miserable and look up for help—it *shall come*. I have travelled twelve years with this load in my heart and this idea in my head. I have gone from door to door of the so-called rich and great. With a bleeding heart I have crossed half the world to this strange land, seeking for help. The Lord is great. I know He will help me. I may perish of cold or hunger in this land, but I bequeath to you, young men, this sympathy, this struggle for the poor, the ignorant, the oppressed. Go now this minute to the temple of Parthasarathi, and before Him who was friend to the poor and lowly cowherds of Gokul, who never shrank to embrace the pariah Guhak, who accepted the invitation of a prostitute in preference to that of the nobles and saved her in His incarnation as Buddha—yea, down on your faces before Him, and make a great sacrifice; the sacrifice of a whole life for them for whom He comes from time to time, whom He loves above all, the poor, the lowly, the oppressed. Vow then to devote your whole lives to the cause of the redemption of these three hundred millions, going down and down every day.

It is not the work of a day, and the path is

full of the most deadly thorns. But Partha-sarathi is ready to be our Sarathi, we know that, and in His name and with eternal faith in Him, set fire to the mountain of misery that has been heaped upon India for ages—and it shall be burned down. Come then, look it in the face, brethren, it is a grand task and we are so low. But we are the sons of Light and Children of God. Glory unto the Lord, we will succeed. Hundreds will fail in the struggle—hundreds will be ready to take it up. I may die here unsuccessful, another will take up the task. You know the disease, you know the remedy, only have faith. Do not look up to the so-called rich and great ; do not care for the heartless intellectual writers, and their cold-blooded newspaper articles. Faith—sympathy, fiery faith, and fiery sympathy ! Life is nothing, death is nothing—hunger nothing, cold nothing. Glory unto the Lord—march on, the Lord is our General. Do not look back to see who falls—forward—onward ! Thus and thus we shall go on, brethern. One falls, and another takes up the work.

OVERLEAF

a list of some books

by and about

Swami Vivekananda

BOOKS BY SWAMI VIVEKANANDA

Selections from Swami Vivekananda

Will be useful to those who cannot afford to read the voluminous *Complete Works (in 7 Vols.)* Pp. 598+ Index, etc. Price Rs. 6.

Lectures from Colombo to Almora

Contains lectures delivered in India and embodying his fiery message for the regeneration of his Motherland. Pp. 416. Price Rs. 5.

Letters of Swami Vivekananda

A nationalist burning with zeal for furthering the cause of the country, a reformer feeling agony at the sight of many defects in the society, a devout religious man longing for the unknown—all will find inspiration from them. 303 in number. Pp. vii+436. Price Rs. 5.

Swami Vivekananda on India and Her Problems

Contains extracts from the Swami's writings and speeches bearing on various Indian problems. Pp. 119. Price Re. 1-8.

Talks with Swami Vivekananda

People in almost all walks of life will find guidance from these pages. Pp. 400. Price Rs. 4.

Thoughts of Power

A collection of thoughts from Swami Vivekananda—to rouse, to inspire and to guide. Pp. 76. Price As. 8

Sadhanas or Preparations for Higher Life

Price As. 5.

Powers of the Mind
Price As. 7.

Work and Its Secret
Price As. 6.

Bhakti or Devotion
Price As. 8.

Poems
Price: Cloth Re. 1-14.
Limp Re. 1-6.

In Defence of Hinduism
Price As. 8.

The East and the West
Price Re. 1.

Practical Vedanta
Price Re. 1-4.

Chicago Addresses
Price As. 6.

Thoughts on the Gita
Price As. 5.

Life after Death
Price As. 8.

Caste, Culture and Socialism
Price Re. 1-4.

My Life and Mission
Price As. 10.

Essentials of Hinduism
Price As. 12.

Modern India
Price As. 10.

Our Women
Price As. 10.

My Master
Price As. 6.

Etc. Etc. Etc.

The Complete Works of Swami Vivekananda
(*In Seven Volumes*)

Price: Each Volume, Board Rs. 6, Cloth Rs. 7-8.

BOOKS ABOUT SWAMI VIVEKANANDA

The Life of Swami Vivekananda

By His Eastern and Western Disciples. Complete in 2 volumes. The only vivid, authentic, all-round and exhaustive biography. Excellent get-up. Demy 8vo. Pp. 500 each volume. Price Rs. 6 each.

The Life of Vivekananda and the Universal Gospel

By Romain Rolland. Translated into English from the original French. Pp. 422. Price Rs. 5-8.

A Short Life of Swami Vivekananda

The present short biography is intended to meet the need of those who, with all their earnestness, have neither the time nor the opportunity to read larger works about the Swami. It is written in a very simple style. Pp. 112. Price Re. 1.